Mercury
The Iron Planet

By Lincoln James

Gareth Stevens
Publishing

Please visit our Web site, www.garethstevens.com. For a free color catalog of all our high-quality books, call toll free 1-800-542-2595 or fax 1-877-542-2596.

Library of Congress Cataloging-in-Publication Data

James, Lincoln.
  Mercury : the iron planet / Lincoln James.
      p. cm. — (Our solar system)
  Includes index.
  ISBN 978-1-4339-3828-3 (pbk.)
  ISBN 978-1-4339-3829-0 (6–pack)
  ISBN 978-1-4339-3827-6 (library binding)
  1. Mercury (Planet)—Juvenile literature. I. Title.
  QB611.J36 2011
  523.41—dc22
                                                    2010000418
First Edition

Published in 2011 by
Gareth Stevens Publishing
111 East 14th Street, Suite 349
New York, NY 10003

Copyright © 2011 Gareth Stevens Publishing

Designer: Christopher Logan
Editor: Greg Roza

Photo credits: Cover, back cover, p. 1 Hulton Archive/Getty Images; pp. 5, 7 courtesy NASA/JPL; pp. 9, 17 Wikimedia Commons; pp. 11, 13, 15, 21 courtesy NASA/JHUAPL; p. 19 (Mercury) De Agostini/Getty Images; p. 19 (iron) Shutterstock.

Printed in the United States of America

CPSIA compliance information: Batch #CS10GS: For further information contact Gareth Stevens, New York, New York at 1-800-542-2595.

Contents

Boldface words appear in the glossary.

The Smallest Planet

Mercury is the smallest planet in our **solar system**. It is also the planet closest to the sun. It is very hot and rocky.

sun

Mars

Venus

Earth

Jupiter

Saturn

Uranus

Neptune

Mercury

Our Solar System

On the Move

All planets spin. Mercury spins very slowly. It takes Mercury about 59 days to turn around just once!

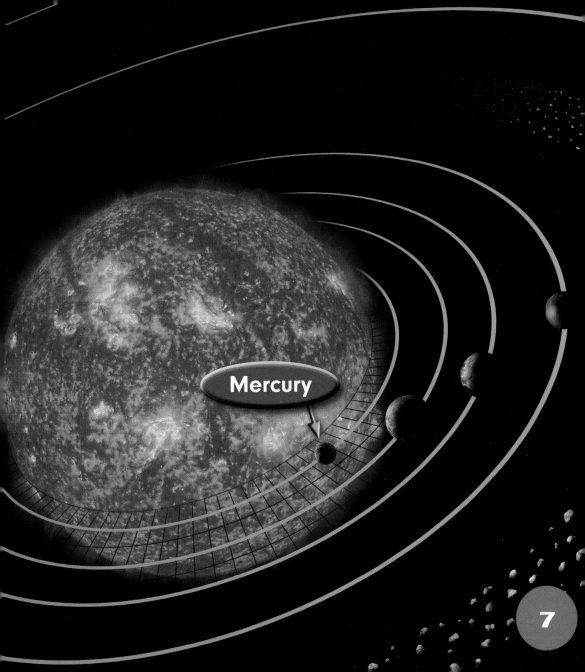

Mercury

All planets **orbit** the sun. Mercury orbits the sun faster than any other planet. Mercury takes just 88 days to go around the sun once.

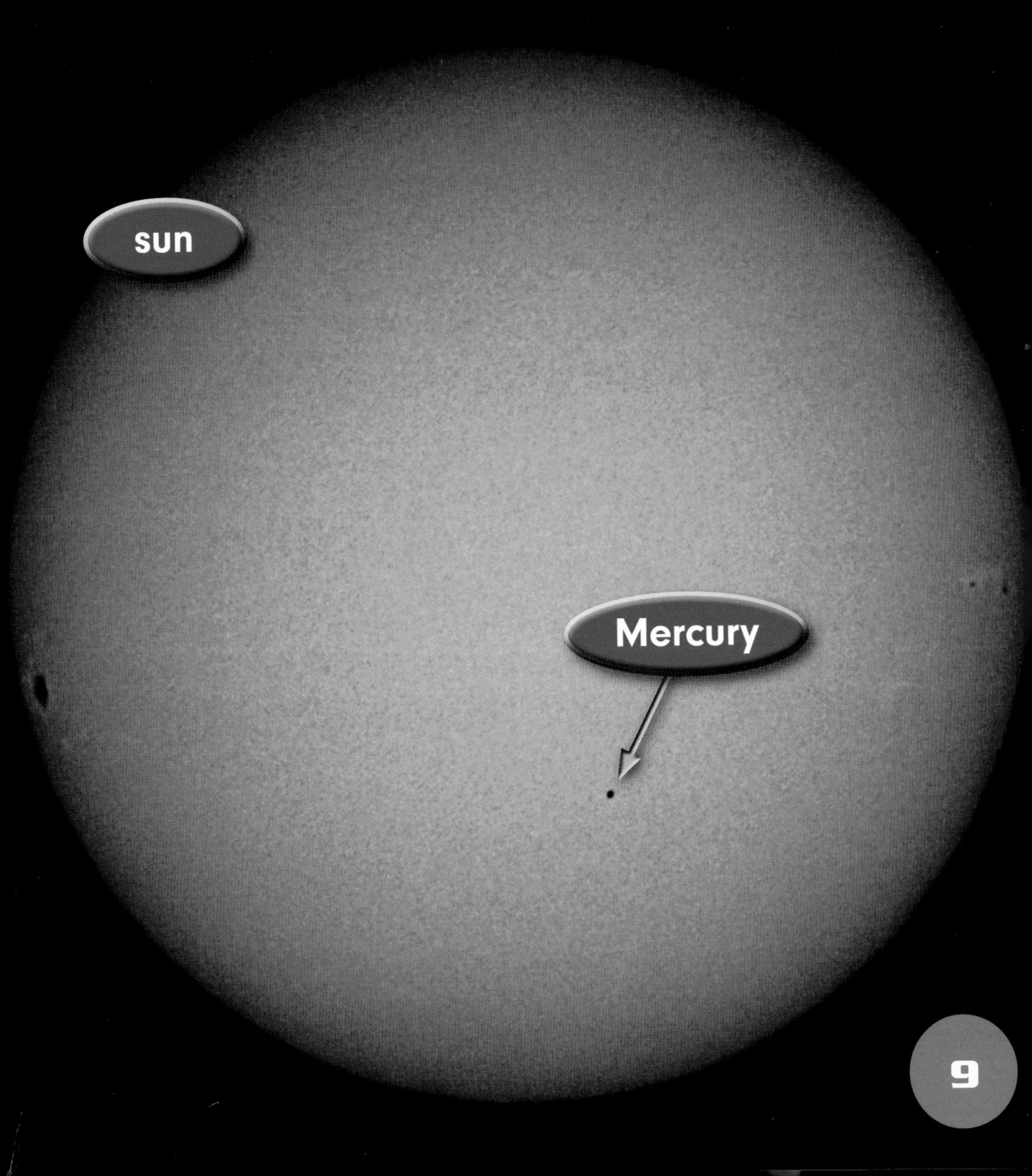
sun
Mercury

No Air There!

Mercury has very little air.
People could never live on
Mercury. There isn't enough
air to breathe.

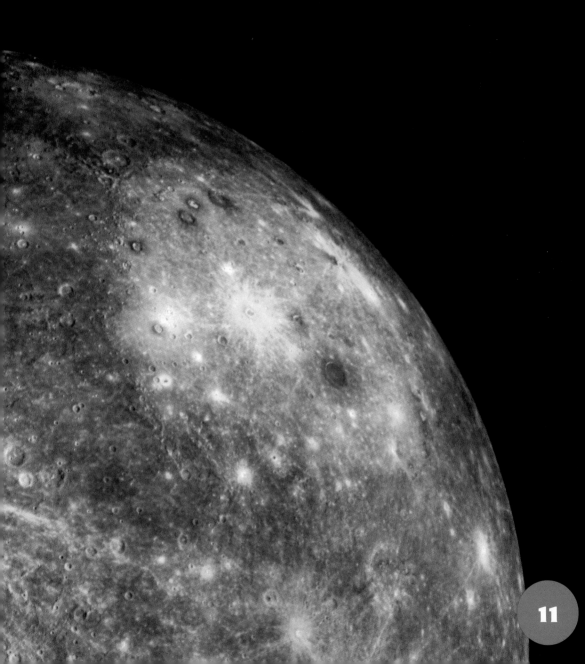

On the Surface

Mercury's **surface** is a lot like the moon's surface. It is made mostly of rock and metals. It is covered in dust.

Just like the moon, Mercury's surface is covered with **craters**. The craters were made when space rocks crashed into Mercury long ago.

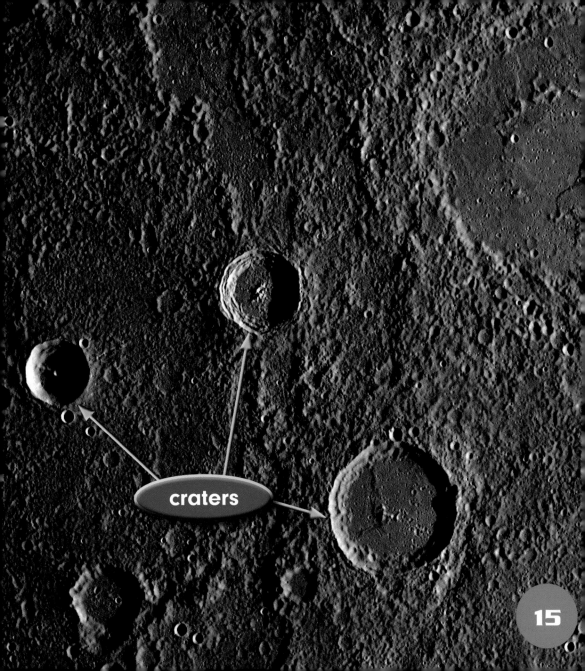

craters

15

Inside Mercury

Mercury is made up of several **layers**. The top layer is called the crust. Below it is a rocky layer called the mantle. The inside is called the core.

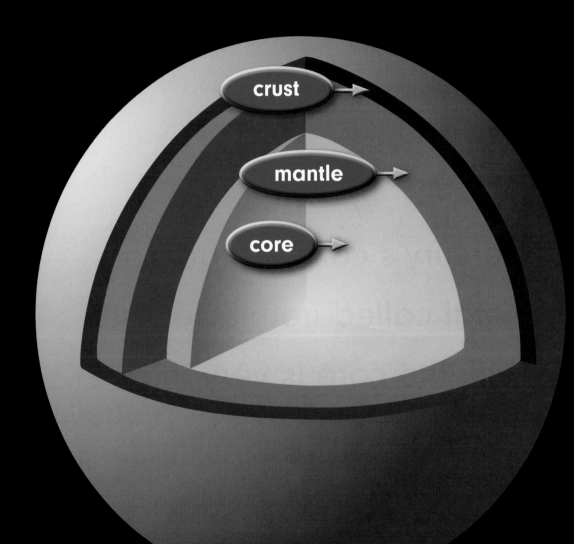

Mercury's core is made of a metal called iron. Scientists think the core is very thick.

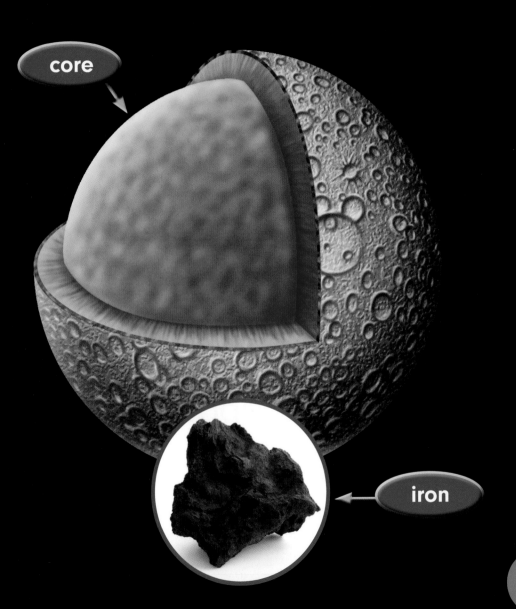

core

iron

Studying Mercury

Scientists have sent several **probes** to study Mercury. Soon, new probes will help us find out more about the sun's closest neighbor.

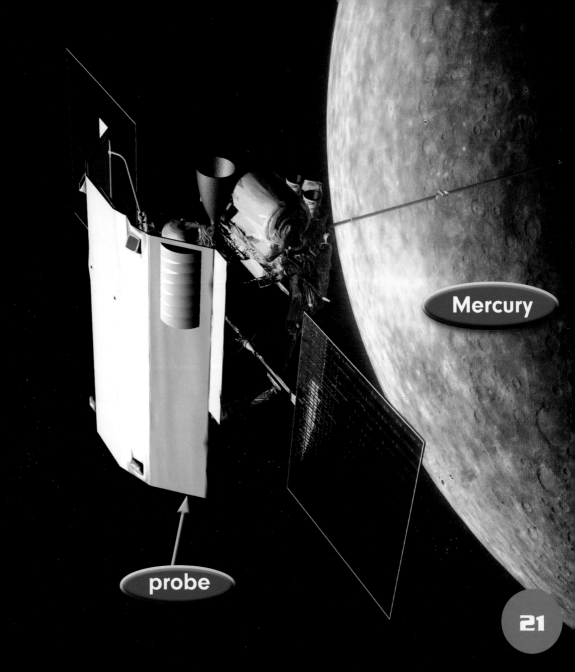

Mercury

probe

Glossary

crater: a bowl-shaped hole on a planet's surface

layer: a single thickness of something lying over or under another

orbit: to travel in a circle or oval around something else

probe: an unmanned spaceship sent to study objects in the solar system

solar system: the sun and all the space objects that orbit it, including the planets and their moons

surface: the top layer of a planet

For More Information

Books

Howard, Fran. *Mercury*. Edina, MN: ABDO, 2007.

Taylor-Butler, Christine. *Mercury*. Danbury, CT: Children's Press, 2008.

Web Sites

Mercury
www.kidsastronomy.com/mercury.htm
Read facts about Mercury and find links to the other planets of the solar system.

Solar System Exploration: Mercury
solarsystem.nasa.gov/planets/profile.cfm?Object=Mercury
NASA's Web page about Mercury includes information about current missions to study the planet.

Index

About the Author

Lincoln James is a retired aerospace engineer and amateur astronomer living in St. Augustine, Florida. He enjoys building miniature rockets with his four sons and taking family trips to the Kennedy Space Center to watch space shuttle launches.